From left, Bob Anderson, John Owen, Rolland Ackermann, Ted Duskin

Big Andy
Tank driver Bob Anderson

A 712th Tank Battalion Interview

By Aaron Elson

Published by:
Chi Chi Press
(888-711-8265)

Other books by Aaron Elson
The Armored Fist: The 712th Tank Battalion in World War 2
A Mile in Their Shoes: Conversations With Veterans of World War 2
Nine Lives: An Oral History
Tanks for the Memories
Merry Christmas in July: B-26 Tail Gunner, ex-POW John Sweren
A Medic's Story

Kassel Mission Interviews
Two Guys Talkin' B-24s
John Cadden
(More coming soon)

http://kasselmission.com
http://www.tankbooks.com
http://oralhistoryaudiobooks.blogspot.com

Bob Anderson
Prophetstown, Illinois
Oct. 24, 1993

Aaron Elson: This is Bob Anderson, also known as Big Andy.

Bob Anderson: I was also known by a lot of other names. Big Stupe. I'll tell you about that later.

3

BOB ANDERSON

Aaron Elson: When did you go into the Army?

Bob Anderson: I went in February 21st, 1941, into the 11th Cavalry.

Aaron Elson: You go back to the cavalry?

Bob Anderson: Oh, yes. I was a horse shoer in the cavalry. I'll show you some pictures back here. My daughter and grandson made a plaque. I went in in '41. I never took basic training because I got in there, and they put a sign on the bulletin board, "Who wants to join the stable gang?" And I was a farmer before I went in. I really wanted to be in the coast artillery. When they asked me at Fort Sheridan what branch of service you'd like, I told them the coast artillery, and I ended up in the horse cavalry. That's how things went back in them days.

I went down there and I was in the stable gang for about, oh, I'm gonna say a couple of weeks or so, and then they wanted to know who wanted to be a horse shoer. And a boy from Chetack, Wisconsin, by the name of Percy Bowers and myself signed up for horse shoeing. Well, instead of going to school we just picked it up right there. Then there was a flip of a coin for who was to be what they called the first horse shoer. It didn't make any difference, we both made shoes – but he was the first horse shoer and I was the second horse shoer.

We got a rating in those days of what we called first-third. That was one stripe down and four turned up. And we were getting paid more than what a buck sergeant was. Of course, we went in at $18 a month, but after we got our rating, we were getting $38 a month, where a sergeant was only getting $36 a month. Then when I came home for my granddad's funeral in October of '41, "Man, look at what a rating he has." Hell, I'm nothing but a Pfc.

I was in the 11th Horse Cavalry. Then the 11th Horse Cavalry and the Third Horse Battalion formed the 10th Armored Division.

4

BOB ANDERSON

Aaron Elson: Clear me up on this, because Forrest Dixon just told me. He said the 11th Cavalry was supposed to go to Australia or to the Philippines. Were you supposed to go to Australia?

Bob Anderson: That's when – see, we were at Campo, California, on the Mexican border, and I didn't know it until later, but when Japan bombed Pearl Harbor they blew boots and saddles and we went down on the Mexican border and sat.

Aaron Elson: Explain to me what it means to blow boots and saddles.

Bob Anderson: Well, that's just a different way of, they didn't yell, they had a bugler, and in the morning he'd blow reveille. And then they'd blow mess call. And there were different calls on the bugle that went out on the air. When they blew boots and saddles, that meant for everybody to run and get ready and go down and saddle your horses, and get ready to ride away.

Aaron Elson: That was immediately? Did you know about Pearl Harbor then, or you just heard boots and saddles?

Bob Anderson: Oh, no. We didn't know. In fact, when Pearl Harbor was bombed, there was a boy named Bud Perkins and myself, and a boy from Wisconsin, Greeley, we had our clothes in the car all ready to come home on a furlough. And before we even got out of camp they blew boots and saddles, and we were confined to camp.

Aaron Elson: Do you remember what kind of car it was?

Bob Anderson: It was a 1939 Ford. I have some pictures of it somewhere. We were going to come home on furlough, but we didn't even get out of camp. Then all the men, and the first horse shoer, they all went down and they had to sleep out and bivouac. Lucky for me, I was the second horse shoer. "You stay back in camp and take care of the stable and feed the horses and take care of them," so I didn't have to go down there and sleep on the ground and all that.

Aaron Elson: Because you lost that coin toss?

Bob Anderson: Well, it's just because I was a very lucky man that I got to stay back in camp. There were about four or five guys got to stay back, and we took care of the horses that were left there. You had 150 men in the troop, and there would be about 180 horses, so there were 30 horses left back there. And then of course at that time we had some sick horses. So I was one of the fortunate ones that didn't have to go down there. But later I did learn, after this, that there was a boat sitting out in the harbor at San Diego that the 11th Cavalry was supposed to go on with their horses and everything and get on this boat, and be in the war, and I wonder how far we'd have gotten fighting the war with the horses in those days. But as luck would have it, in May of '42, well, I'd have to get my book, there was a black unit came in and took over our horses and the white boys were sent to Fort Benning, Georgia, and the 3rd Horse Cavalry, which was stationed up around Washington, D.C., came to Fort Benning and we all formed the 10th Armored Division.

Aaron Elson: Going back to the cavalry, Forrest Dixon said there was something about a yellow fever vaccination, where a lot of men came down with jaundice.

Bob Anderson: I came down with spinal meningitis. I had yellow jaundice before, when I was in high school. The only thing I remember about it was when I had this spinal meningitis, they quarantined the camp for a few days. But anyway, I was sent up to a naval base.

BOB ANDERSON

Aaron Elson: One other question about the cavalry. Was there a horse named Old Buck? Does that ring a bell?

Bob Anderson: There were several horses. We had different names for different things. We had Johnson Bar. Yes, I suppose there was.

Aaron Elson: Ed Stuever said there was a horse there that rode in the campaign against Pancho Villa, and it was out to pasture and given special treatment.

Bob Anderson: It could have been. I can't tell you anything like that. There were special horses the lieutenants had, or I wouldn't say the lieutenants, the officers had their horses and we had to treat them like, well, let's say gold or silver, a little bit better, and they rode with saddles, where we had the old McCulloch saddle they got to ride with the English saddle. And then they had their "dogrobbers" who took care of their stuff, where we had to take care of our own. But I really enjoyed the cavalry. One thing I will say about the outfit I was in, we grew up as a group of men that stayed together. I can list several of us that stayed together and went through the 10th Armored, and went to the 712th Tank Battalion, we fought together and we came home together. And there's a lot of boys that did that. Earl Apgar lives up here in Rockford. Jule Braatz lives up here in Beaver Dam. And there were several boys out of Chicago I can name, and we all stayed together after we got out. We became brothers, like you said this Quentin Bynum, shucks, him and I we fought and had one heck of a good time. This Percy Bowers from Chetack, Wisconsin, who was killed overseas, we were the best of buddies. I will say I went all the way through the service, I got three Bronze Stars, had tanks knocked out. With my luck I never got a Purple Heart. That kind of, it just gets you, now.

After we left the horse cavalry we formed the 10th Armored Division. From the 10th Armored Division we went onto the Tennessee

7

maneuvers. Then we came back to Fort Benning and we were busted away from the 10th Armored Division to the 712th Tank Battalion. From there we went to Camp Gordon, Georgia.

Aaron Elson: At what point did you become a driver?

Bob Anderson: You want a good story there. When I was a horse shoer back in the cavalry, we had a stable sergeant whose name was Seeney. We were way down here, probably a half a mile from the barracks, and the only way you could get a pass to go into town was to be in uniform. Well, the stable gang, they got to eat breakfast at 5 in the morning, 11 o'clock at noon, and 5 o'clock in the evening. And then an hour later the company came. Well, this was one Saturday noon, we came up and ate dinner. And I went into the orderly room to get a pass to go to town, this Percy Bowers and I wanted to come to town and buy a car. Well, Sergeant Chin was in charge of quarters, and him and I was razzin', going at each other. Chin says, "You know you've got to be in uniform."

I says, "Sergeant Chin, how can I get down there and get in uniform and come back up and get a pass before the rest of the company comes in and gets their passes?"

We were just having a lot of fun. Well, in walked – when we first went in Sergeant Gaines was our first sergeant, he was a heck of a good man. After Pearl Harbor he left and went to OCS school and became a captain in the MPs. A Sergeant Moseley took over who had been back at Fort Riley, Kansas, an officers' school, and got to be first sergeant. Well, Moseley walked in the orderly room while Chin and I was at it, and he just says, "You know the orders around here." You know, being he was the top soldier. And I hauled off and hit him one. So the next day it was Pfc. Third Class Specialist Robert E. Anderson was busted to a grade of Pfc. returned to duty. In other words, I was kicked out of the stable and sent back there.

8

BOB ANDERSON

Aaron Elson: You hit him?

Bob Anderson: Yeah, I hit him. I was mad. So about a week later he was shipped out and Sergeant Seeney, who was the stable sergeant, was next in rank, he got to be first sergeant, so I got to go back down to the stable. We were known as Seeney's boys. Seeney went with us to the 10th Armored Division, and everybody who was down in the stable gang, they got to be tank drivers. So that's how we did. Bowers, Bynum, [Lano] O'Conner, [Dess] Tibbetts, all of us got to be tank drivers. Of course, a tank driver, they didn't have to stand guard duty or do KP, they had to take care of the tanks. So we were known as Seeney's boys.

Aaron Elson: Your rank as a tank driver was a corporal?

Bob Anderson: No, my rank, see, I drove what they call the three, I was in the third platoon and drove the third tank. So the one that was in each platoon that drove the No. 1 tank, they drove the lieutenant. I drove the staff sergeant's tank, so I was in the third platoon driving the third tank. So each driver there got what they call a T-4 rating. The other drivers were a T-5 or a corporal rating. There were two sergeant drivers and two corporal drivers.

Aaron Elson: The platoon leader was a lieutenant. The platoon sergeant...

Bob Anderson: Was a staff sergeant.

Aaron Elson: Okay, was in the fourth tank?

Bob Anderson: Yes. They were supposed to, if you go into combat – when we went into combat you threw the book away. Three tanks were supposed to go up, and then these two tanks were supposed to advance,

9

and then ... but when we went into action we threw the book away. I'll get to that story a little later. But anyway, after we went to Camp Gordon, we got sent up to Myles Standish, that's where we shipped out for England. Then when we were in England, we did a lot of training, and there was a boy by the name [L.E.] Stahl, he was a sergeant tank driver like I was. We were welding on the tanks one night and got the dickens for doing that because we were lighting the sky, you know how a welder will light it up. We were working on our tanks one night. The Germans weren't flying over but if they had been flying over they'd have seen us. Well, we got there, and then we stayed there for quite a while, and then we went down to the port of Southampton and went across to Omaha Beach. And I had this sergeant by the name Charles Fowler from California, and he was a soldier in the States. A well-built man and that. But when he got into action, he was scared. And he admitted it. Finally, he'd tell me not to start the tank. Gunner don't load your gun. This and that. Finally, I went to the company commander and told him what was going on. Fowler was busted to a grade of a private or a Pfc, I don't know which, and shipped back to the States. But he admitted he was scared, which was a good thing, you know, he was more dangerous to his men being scared.

Aaron Elson: Ruby Goldstein told me there was something where Fowler said there were branches in the turret.

Bob Anderson: Well, you didn't know what. Reuben Goldstein was in the same platoon, and he was in the tank back of us. In fact, his driver was Ringwalski from Minnesota. He was in the tank behind us, and him and this Charlie Bahrke got the first award issued in our outfit. Charlie Bahrke was the gunner and Goldstein was the tank commander and they each got a Silver Star. The way they did it is, I don't know, did they tell you about a hedgerow?

BOB ANDERSON

Aaron Elson: He described a hedgerow, but he never said he got the Silver Star for that.

Bob Anderson: Oh yeah, he got, anyway, when you come up over these here hedgerows – we didn't know it, we did after the first one – but anyway, we was coming through this field and we come up over a hedgerow like that and we just dropped. Probably about, oh, I'd say six, eight feet deep. And here he was sitting right in here. And then I had to maneuver and all of us drivers had to maneuver our tanks, jockey them around to get headed down the road.

Aaron Elson: Goldstein's tank had fallen over the hedgerow?

Bob Anderson: Yes. But Goldstein got jockeyed around, and they went down the road a short distance, and they was hit with an anti-tank gun. The crew evacuated the tank, and then Goldstein and Bahrke crawled back with the protection of the tank, and we've got a hatch in the bottom of the tank, they crawled back up in there, and got the anti-tank gun that was down at the end of the road. And that's how they got the Silver Star.

Aaron Elson: Was that the very first day?

Bob Anderson: Well, I won't say the first day, but it was close to the first day. I'd say the first week. The first day, and I don't know if they ever mentioned it, we hadn't been in, I'll say action, I'll say an hour, when Lieutenant [George] Tarr out of the second platoon and another boy out of Headquarters Company by the name of Phil Schromm, they were the first two men in our outfit who got killed.

Aaron Elson: I've heard several stories about how Tarr was killed. See, my father was supposed to replace Tarr.

11

BOB ANDERSON

Bob Anderson: Oh, he came in right early.

Aaron Elson: He reported to Braatz, and Braatz said he was showing him the tank, and he told my father to be careful getting off, and my father jumped off and sprained his foot and went to the medics, and then the tanks went into action without him. [Sgt. Jule Braatz was the first of 14 sergeants in the 712th to receive a battlefield commission.]

Bob Anderson: See, George Tarr, he was Braatz's platoon leader, and I can't help but believe that every time, see, then your sergeant would move up to the Number One. Every time Braatz would get a replacement, just within a week or maybe not that long, something would happen that this lieutenant would get hurt or wounded, so Braatz would have to take over. Finally they offered Braatz a lieutenant rating and he was commissioned in the field.

We had a, well, I call them 90-day wonders, maybe I shouldn't, these were men that came out of the States, and came over and tried to tell us boys how we should fight and this and that. I had a Lieutenant Bell...

Aaron Elson: I was talking to John McDaniel at the reunion and he was talking about Lieutenant Bell. He said he was an oddball.

Bob Anderson: That's what I say. I had, here's a picture of a man right here, he was my assistant driver after he came in and replaced a driver. I don't know what rank he had in the infantry but he had to do something else. His name was John C. Owens. And he came in and he was trying to tell us how to drive a tank and how to do this and that. He was my assistant driver. It ended up that one day – well, I'll get to that later on. Then I lost another buddy of mine, this Percy Bowers. He was killed at Avranches.

He was killed in a cemetery. His tank was knocked out. Pretty near

12

all of us was out of ammunition. His tank was knocked out, he got out of his tank and was carrying a white flag, crawling back, and some German shot him, with a white flag, crawling back. That's where he was killed.

Aaron Elson: Other people in Percy Bowers' tank were killed also, weren't they?

Bob Anderson: Well, there were. See, Percy Bowers was in the first platoon. I can't tell you.

Aaron Elson: And [Harry] Bell was your platoon leader?

Bob Anderson: Well, first I had Lieutenant [Ed] Forrest.

Aaron Elson: What was he like?

Bob Anderson: He was a very good man. He was just a common, ordinary man. He was with us all the way. I liked him. All the officers we had when we went over, you didn't have to go around and salute them, even the big shot, [Col. Vladimir] Kedrovsky, after he took over from Randolph [Col. George B. Randolph was killed during the Battle of the Bulge], Colonel Kedrovsky was just an ordinary man. He knew me when we came along, and it was Big Andy this and Big Andy that. When we had our first reunion in Rockford he was there, and him and I sat and talked a long time.

Aaron Elson: Was Steve Krysko in your tank?

Bob Anderson: He was in our outfit. Now, here's where I got my first Bronze Star, in Dillingen. I was the first tank across. The engineers had laid down our bridge, and we were sitting on the bank waiting to go across, and they came back and they said, "Now, when you go across, go slow." Well, you know how it is with a 32-ton tank going across water. As I was going across, I was probably three-quarters of the way across or so, two German planes came in and started strafing across the river. And you ought to have seen me go across the river. I didn't go slow. Anyway, the two tanks behind me got mired down. Our third platoon, we got all five tanks across, but two of them got mired down out in the mud. I took my tank, and we had cables, oh, I might say 15, 20 feet long. I hooked three of them together and dragged them back, and hooked onto the tank back there in the mire, and then I went and got back in my tank, and I got the two tanks pulled back out.

Aaron Elson: Who hooked up the cables?

Bob Anderson: I did. Some of the others didn't know how to hook up a cable. I hooked the cables together and got these two tanks out that were mired in the mud, and that's how I got my first Bronze Star. Of course, I pulled my tank, we got in there right up in front of a store and we looted that.

Now this is the picture that they took of me cutting this meat up. They sent a great big one which I've got in a frame, they sent that back to my wife. And then Lieutenant [Ray] Griffin, I don't know how he got hold of that, but he sent that to me. This John C. Owens, he was my assistant driver. It says that I killed a cow with a broken leg, well, it didn't have no more of a broken leg than you and I when I shot that cow. This Owens, later, we had orders one night to move out, and I'm trying to think who our company commander was. I know [Bob] Hagerty was my tank commander.

Aaron Elson: Could it have been George Coulton?

Bob Anderson: No, Coulton was a driver. You're thinking of George Cozzens. Him and I tangled two, three times. He could have

14

been. But anyway they told me – see, I wasn't going to move out that night. Anyway, this Cozzens told us that we had to move out to a certain place that night, and I said, "No, I'm not going to go. I'm not taking these tanks, my tank, out after dark." And him and I went round and round and he assured me that there was nothing down this road in front of them pillboxes, that they were all clear. And I can't think who else was in on it. I know Hagerty was there. He was the platoon leader. No he wasn't the platoon leader. Because I was still driving the third platoon tank.

Aaron Elson: Do you remember where this was?

Bob Anderson: Oberwampach, that's where this happened. We got down this road, and the first tank got hit with a bazooka, and the last tank got hit with a bazooka. And then the three in between. I got a bazooka in the gas tank of my tank. We went to evacuate our tank and got out, and this Owens, we had to go up a hill, and we were going up this hill, then the Germans, why they didn't shoot us when we got out of our tank I'll never know. Anyway, we got going up this hill and this Owens was hit with shrapnel. And I picked him up on my shoulder and I must have carried him a half, three-quarters of a mile and all he could say is "I'm hit in my head, I'm hit in the head," and his ass was so full of shrapnel that you've never seen anything like it. But I carried him back to the first aid.

Aaron Elson: Was he hit in the head?

Bob Anderson: No, it's just that he was in such pain. That's where I got my second Bronze Star. Well, like a darn fool, I went back and grabbed a fire extinguisher and went down and tried to put the fire out in my tank, that's just how stupid I was. I seen the Germans standing right there, just like they were about from here to that shed up there, away from me. Why they didn't shoot me I don't know.

15

BOB ANDERSON

Aaron Elson: Were there many of them?

Bob Anderson: Oh yes, there was a lot of them. Now why did I grab that, that's just how I felt. This is a true story, this ain't no bull. Why did I take that and go down there and try to put a fire out with a little fire extinguisher in a 32-ton tank.

Aaron Elson: And the rest of the crew had left?

Bob Anderson: Well, they were standing up on the hill. It's just that way. That was in the Battle of the Bulge, but then I got my third Bronze Star in Branscheid. So really, the most important thing that I remember after the Battle of the Bulge was when we took this Merkers mine. [A vast hoard of Nazi treasure was hidden in the Merkers salt mine.] I was the first tank in there. I won't say the infantry wasn't, but I was the first tank in there, driving the first tank. And as we pulled in there was a train leaving. And my gunner, Ted Duskin, of course the train was going fast, so we started running alongside or trying to catch it, and Duskin put a shell right in the engine and blew it up. Well, we pulled back to the mine and we sat there until I don't know how long, not knowing what was in it. We didn't know for two or three days after how wealthy some of us could have been.

I'll say this much, Ted Duskin was, I don't know whether he was a hillbilly, but he didn't get all the credit he deserved. He was self-conscious. He took care of that gun like, if I don't have that gun clean and this and that, it's my life. He was very good about taking care of the gun, and he was a real good worker. I loved Ted Duskin. But he was sort of like, he came out of Virginia, but it was like he came out of the mountains, or the backwoods. Now here it says he was a private. I think he had a corporal rating. Because he was a very good man. But then it went on for a while, and then I was sent home – no, our company headquarters were bombed – I was sent back into maintenance then. And

16

BOB ANDERSON

I'd been working up on the line, changing plugs and things like that. I came in one night, it was 10:30 or 11 o'clock, and they came in and they said, "Is Anderson here?"

I said "What do you want?"

"Do you want a tech sergeant rating, or do you want to go home?"

I thought they were joking with me when they said that. I said, "I want to go home."

"All right, be ready to leave in 15 minutes."

I said, "Bullshit, I'm going to bed. I'm tired."

Then in came Kedrovsky. He said, "Well, Anderson, you're entitled, you've got points, and you can go home."

Then here comes Cozzens with some messages, for me to do this. Lieutenant [Ken] Fisher comes, "Here's some money, you take home for me." Another one, "You take home and send that."

Anyway, I came home on a boat and there was a thousand Germans and 13 enlisted men. And this lieutenant, Ray Griffin, I didn't know him at the time but he was on that boat.

We got home – well, five days out of York V-E Day came, and of the course the Germans, they all were going to marry American ladies and they were going to go to school.

I finally got home, and there was a telephone call from a Mrs. Cozzens. So when I landed in New York I called and gave them the messages. Cozzens had me do it. Instead I gave the wrong message to the wrong woman. Here was this lady, she had called my wife in Nebraska, of course I lived in Illinois, but she called my wife in Nebraska and said, "This is Mrs. Cozzens." She wanted me to call her, gave her name and everything. When I got home we were out to Nebraska, somebody said, "Your cousins called you." Cousins?

So anyway, this Mrs. Cozzens called. I called her. She said, "Where's George?" And all this and that. I told her. But I told her the wrong message. He ended up divorced. Then I learned from other men, I guess he had women all over.

17

BOB ANDERSON

Aaron Elson: Tell me about the third Bronze Star. These are the citations for the Bronze Star. "For heroic service in support of operations against the enemy during the period 9 to 10 December, 1944, in the vicinity of" – that would be Dillingen – "when the tanks of a platoon were mired in the marshy soil on the far side of the river, Technician 4th Grade Anderson, tank driver, with companions, subjected himself to heavy enemy artillery and mortar fire and labored arduously to retrieve the tanks. His untiring efforts and complete devotion to duty were instrumental in saving the tanks and in enabling the platoon to accomplish its mission. His heroic service was in accordance with military tradition.

"First oak leaf cluster. For heroic service in support of operation from 15 to 19 January, 1945, in the vicinity of" – you had said where that was, that was Oberwampach? [A Company of the 712th and a company from the 90th Infantry Division withstood between seven and nine counterattacks between Jan. 18 and 19 at Oberwampach, Luxembourg].

Bob Anderson: Yes.

Aaron Elson: "... After helping to take the town, the tank crew of which Technician 4th Grade Anderson was a member repelled seven counterattacks. Technician 4th Grade Anderson in his capacity as driver maneuvered his tank expertly to aid materially in destroying several hostile tanks and killing or wounding numerous enemy. His heroic service was in accordance with military tradition."

And the second oak leaf cluster. "For heroic service in support of operations on 7 February 1945 in the vicinity of Branscheid, Germany. The tank which Technician 4th Grade Anderson was driving was struck and set ablaze by bazooka fire. Despite heavy enemy fire and the proximity of hostile troops, Technician 4th Grade Anderson obtained an extinguisher and attempted to put out the blaze. Later, upon returning to friendly lines, he helped evacuate a wounded comrade to an aid station. His heroic service was in accordance with military tradition." Now that sounds like what you were describing as Oberwampach.

Bob Anderson: Yeah, I'm ahead of myself, I was. See, Oberwampach is what you were referring to. And this was later. I was ahead of myself.

Aaron Elson: So Oberwampach is where...

Bob Anderson: I maneuvered the tank. And then the last time...

Aaron Elson: Now tell me about Oberwampach, what you remember.

Bob Anderson: Well, like I say, all I remember is it was severe fighting. I had several chances of being tank commander and all that, getting a staff sergeant rating, but I felt safer down there driving. To me, a driver was more important than a tank commander. Sure, a tank commander gave the orders, but still you had to have a man down there who knew how to maneuver them tanks. And I think going back to all the boys that I know, Bynum, Stahl, [Edmund] Pilz, Bowers, and all the drivers we had, George Bussell out of Indianapolis, Ringwalski, I think we all were a very good bunch of drivers. Other companies would have felt the same way about their drivers.

But now, you go back to this time up in the Ardennes when this Quentin Bynum, better known as Pine Valley, when he got killed. If they would have – they had a new lieutenant.

Aaron Elson: His name was Lippincott.

Bob Anderson: That's right. You know more of these details...

19

BOB ANDERSON

Aaron Elson: Hagerty told me.

Bob Anderson: This Lippincott, I heard it all over the intercom – they were in this forest, and the Germans were laying artillery, and the shrapnel was coming down and hitting the tank. And this Lippincott said "Abandon tank."

And Bynum said, "No, Lieutenant, that's just shrapnel. Just sit still."

"I said abandon tank."

And they all abandoned tank but one man, his name was Shaginobe or something like that, he was an Indian [Frank Shagonabe]. And he stayed in the tank, and he's the only live boy out of that crew [actually, Shagonabe, Bynum and Lieutenant Wallace Lippincott were killed, while two crew members, Hilton Chiasson and Roy La Pish, survived]. I don't know why Bynum obeyed – but this Lippincott, if he would have listened to an older man, they all might have been alive today. As it was, about two or three days later, they asked me if I'd go back and identify Bynum.

Aaron Elson: How badly was he disfigured?

Bob Anderson: I would just say you could recognize the man. He was full of shrapnel, and laying in the snow. Of course he had his clothes on. A few years ago I went down and saw some of his folks, and his mother – I don't know why I didn't go down there when we first came out – his mother didn't believe in burying him underground, he's buried on top of the ground [in a mausoleum]. She had him brought back. Now I went up to Chetack, Wisconsin, to see Bowers' folks. They didn't have him brought back. When I was back in Germany, it must have been about 17 years ago, I did go to Bowers' grave.

Aaron Elson: I've seen a photograph of it. Let me ask you, do you recall the fight that broke out in the middle of the night?

BOB ANDERSON

Bob Anderson: I know what you're talking about, when Sergeant Martin got his arm blew off?

Aaron Elson: No, no. I want to hear about that. That was a different one. That was Mainz. Let's do that. That was at Mainz.

Bob Anderson: Right. I just got off guard that night. Back in them days, the lieutenant, no matter who he was, when you're up on the line, stood a guard. I'd just gotten off guard, I was in my tank. The 773rd T.D.s [tank destroyers] were off to our right, across the road in another, well, we called them a yard, but anyway there was a fence and all. This Sergeant Martin, Lloyd Martin, he wouldn't go in the barn and sleep. He stayed in his tank. And he kept the breech open.

I had just got off guard, I hadn't even got in bed yet, in my sleeping bag or whatever it was, and we heard this shooting out in the yard. And I took my tommy gun and I came down the stairsteps shooting all the way. I got out in the yard, I got over to my tank, got into it, and I maneuvered it around in such a way that my gunner got in with me...

Aaron Elson: That was Duskin?

Bob Anderson: Duskin. And we did fire. Whether we hit any tanks coming in or any Germans I can't say, because the T.D.s were firing this way and we were firing that way. It's a wonder we didn't hit one another. But when it was clear, said and done, we went over to the tank, and they had thrown a potato masher up in the gun, in the 76 of Martin's tank, and he had his breech open, and some way or other, he had his hand right in front of that, it blew his hand off just about up to here. I never did hear from him or anything like that, but he was a boy from California, and when we were in the horse cavalry together we had a dog we called Big Red. It was a red dog, I won't say a spaniel, it was a bigger dog than that.

21

BOB ANDERSON

He kept that dog and he took it with us to the 10th Armored, and he took it on the Tennessee maneuvers with him, and I don't know when he gave the dog up, but he made friends with that dog and had the dog all the time. But that was the time when he got his hand blew off. If he hadn't had the breech open on his gun, I'll say that he wouldn't have lost his arm.

Aaron Elson: Was that standard procedure to leave the breech open?

Bob Anderson: No. I suppose they had been cleaning the gun before we quit that night, but you see, the Germans, their tanks were awful quiet running, and the infantry was a good 80 rods or so ahead of us dug in for the night. How it was that – there were three or four German tanks came in – how them tanks got by that infantry line, I don't know, because they surprised us. There was a counterattack at night, I would say somewhere around 1 or 2 o'clock.

Then there was one time when, the worst one I ever, that was bad but the worst deal I ever had, that I was really mad, and that was when we'd been up on the front lines and we came back into bivouac, were into a rest area that night, my tanks were empty on gas, and didn't have a round of ammunition, and we, I'm trying think of this man from Service Company, I thought it started with an S, because Dixon and I were just talking about him the other day, he was a truck driver. Well, anyway, he hauled our gas, and he pulled up to me, and he said, "How many gallons today, Big Andy?"

And I said, "A hundred and seventy five."

Well, he dumped it off on the ground. And the next guy pulled up and he says, "How many rounds of ammunition?"

And Duskin told him, I can't tell you just how many went in the tank, he told him he wanted a full supply. So I started in. I had 15 gallons of gas dumped in the tank, and Duskin was starting to clean the gun. The tank commanders and the rest of them had pulled the hatches down and they were making coffee. They weren't helping. And in drove three tanks, German tanks, and they just wiped our kitchen crew right out. You know, the kitchen crew was up ahead. I jumped in the tank and we took off and ran. And my tank commander and I had quite a few words after that. And he admitted that he was – of course that always put me against drinking coffee. Of course, I never drink coffee myself. But what the heck is that guy doing? But anyway, that was one experience I had.

Aaron Elson: Was that at the Falaise Gap?

Bob Anderson: I can't tell you where it was at. But that was one thing that stuck in my mind for a long time, it still does. I'm not gonna mention any names. I know, I kind of hold that against that sonofa ... I think if we'd have had a round or two of ammunition in the tank or something we could have maybe knocked a German tank out or saved maybe a few men up in the headquarters company. But I wish I could think of that man's name, he drove a truck.

Aaron Elson: Tell me about the attack that broke out in the middle of the night.

Bob Anderson: I don't remember, I can't...

Aaron Elson: That's the one in the history book, with the map. There's a drawing of it. I know some A Company tanks were involved. At Mairy. Neal Vaughn told me about it. Bell was the platoon leader at the time.

Bob Anderson: To be honest with you, I can't remember that. I just don't remember that. 90th Division C.P. No, I couldn't tell you anything about that.

BOB ANDERSON

Aaron Elson: Do you remember the Falaise Gap?

Bob Anderson: That was, I remember the Falaise Gap, was that down there when that railroad car loaded with black powder?

Aaron Elson: That was at the end of the war. The Falaise Gap was just after Avranches.

Bob Anderson: I remember the Falaise Gap. I can't remember anything about that.

Aaron Elson: Was Sam Cropanese in your platoon?

Bob Anderson: I remember him. He was in a different platoon. I do remember the town of Metz. That's when we first got Cozzens. And he got in the tank retriever, and he had a boy who's gone now, Joe, gosh, I'm getting so I can't even remember names, Joe Medich, we called him Moose Medich, Cozzens had him drive up through town, and Braatz got on the C.B., he says, "Where are you, Cozzens?" And he said "I'm way up here," or something. Braatz says, "Turn that goddamn tank around and get the hell back, you're way in front of the lines. It's a wonder you ain't shot." But Cozzens, thinking he knew everything, he just got in that tank and had Medich take him up through there and they didn't even have a gun on the tank, that was a tank retriever, and I remember that was when we first got Cozzens. He was an oddball. He was crazy as the dickens.
Have you talked to Braatz?

Aaron Elson: Years ago, before I really started this.

Bob Anderson: Have you ever talked to Howard Olsen? Hagerty and [Morse] Johnson would be able to help you a lot.

24

Aaron Elson: Yes, they did, tremendously. Tell me about the cold during the Bulge.

Bob Anderson: Oh, gosh, I know it was cold, and a lot of snow and that. I would say it was weather like we have right in here, summer it's hot, winter it was times when it got down to ten below, twenty below zero. Now when we moved from Dillingen up through Luxembourg, I know it was cold because I took and cut a sock up and just made a slit for my eyes to see and I covered my head. That was quite an experience there. I didn't have an assistant tank driver and I was getting sleepy and one time I hit an icy spot in the road, and I sat on the edge of a cliff, just about like that, and the tank rocking, and going over, and just a laughing, and Hagerty, he said, "What's the matter?" And I said, "Well, we're just about ready to go over the cliff." A guy came up behind me and hooked his tank on and pulled me back. And then there was another time I ran General Patton off the road. I stopped. He said, "You did the right thing, Soldier. You had the road. Get them tanks up there." And then another time I hit an icy spot and damn near went through a building, and then we pulled the tank back and we helped other tanks. That was cold that night and the road was icy and it was snowing.

Aaron Elson: You traveled all night?

Bob Anderson: We traveled all night. I think we left around 9, 10 o'clock at night and I think we had to be up [near] Bastogne around 6 o'clock in the morning. It was an all-night affair and you didn't drive with lights, you drove in the blind. It was quite a trip.

Aaron Elson: How steep was that cliff you almost went over?

Bob Anderson: That I don't know. We were just sitting there like that. It could have been just a ditch or it could have been a mountain. See,

25

BOB ANDERSON

Luxembourg is quite hilly, and I don't know that, I just remember that I sat on the edge and the tank was rocking, whether the tank was far enough out that if you had put a 50-pound weight on the gun it would have gone over I couldn't say. Like I say, I was so cold and sleepy, and I didn't have an assistant driver to take over and drive for a while.

Aaron Elson: What happened to the assistant driver?

Bob Anderson: I don't remember, well, now wait a while. It seemed to me the assistant driver I started out with was moved up into my tank, his name was Williamson, and he was the loader on the gun then. See, they started changing men around after certain ones got injured. Say that you had a good gunner, and maybe a tank commander got wounded, they'd take this gunner and make him a tank commander. They'd take the assistant driver and maybe make him a driver. I don't know just how things got moving around. But like I say, I started out with Fowler, and then I had E.E. Crawford. And then I had Lieutenant Bell, and then I had Hagerty. Sergeant Fowler, and then it was E.E. Crawford, and then Bell, and then Hagerty. Those were the four main tank commanders I had. Of course Hagerty got commissioned in the field so I moved from the third tank up to the first tank, but generally I was in the third tank in the platoon.

Aaron Elson: Some people have said that the platoon sergeant rode in the fourth tank, that there were three tanks in the first section.

Bob Anderson: That's true, have I been telling you...

Aaron Elson: You would have been in the fourth tank.

Bob Anderson: You're right. There were three tanks, one, two and three were in the first section. And the four and five tank were supposed

26

to cover the first three tanks according to the book as they moved up.

Aaron Elson: You said the book was thrown out.

Bob Anderson: Well, that's what you learned, the way you were supposed to fight the war. You know, after you get over there and get to seeing things, you look after yourself and look after somebody else. Well, just like I say, these three tanks were supposed to advance and then these two tanks here advance, well heck, you know, you used your common sense. You used your own judgment.

Aaron Elson: What do you recall about direct confrontations with tiger tanks, or the German tanks?

Bob Anderson: Well, I'll say this, when we first went into action we had what we called a 75-millimeter gun, and we might just as well have had a BB-gun. You actually could shoot that 75-millimeter gun against a German tank and see the projectile just jump off. Then finally we got what we called a 76, and that did penetrate. And then a little later on they finally gave us a 90-millimeter. But the only way, when we first went into action, is when we hit a German tank, you either hit their tracks – we found this out – you either shoot for their tracks, or right around the edge of the turret there's a ring, do that. I think, too, that the first time we were in action and our projectile hit a German tank, I would say 25 percent of the time the Germans were as scared as we were, just jumped out of the tank thinking their guns were hit. Because really, I know, and the rest of the people, them 75s weren't worth a damn against the German tanks as far as piercing, the armor-piercing. But after we got the 76 and then the 90-millimeter, then we had a chance. And I'll give the Germans a lot of credit, their tanks were diesel, where ours were gas, and a German tank was much more quieter creeping up on us. Also, they would turn a lot shorter. We'd have to take a, well, I'll say just an acre of ground where

27

they could turn around on a dime. The Germans were way ahead of us at the start of the war, if they knew it. But we had artillery and we had the superior air power, and we had a heck of a good infantry, and that's what did it. As far as the tanks, I don't know why they sent our tanks into France, or Normandy, with the 75s after we had been in Africa fighting. Patton should have known that them 75 guns were no good against the German tanks. Now why that wasn't down there, because Rommel, they had enough tanks fighting down there, maybe they didn't have 75s, maybe they had good tanks in Africa.

Aaron Elson: Tell me again about this photograph. This was a cow that...

Bob Anderson: Well, I just went out and shot a cow, because I'd been on a farm and I'd butchered and this and that. We wanted some steak.

Aaron Elson: What would you normally eat when you were out in the field?

Bob Anderson: Generally we had what we called C rations, that was a can of, oh, Spam and crackers and that. And the first thing we did when we got into any homes or any town or somewhere, why you'd grab the eggs. I had a lot of cases of eggs I lost on the front. They had the eggs, the French people and the Germans would have the eggs hid under the beds. You'd get the eggs.

Aaron Elson: What do you mean by a lot of cases of eggs that you lost?

Bob Anderson: Well, I'd find – not just me but all of us would find, what we did, was on the front of these tanks we'd put a plank, and then

28

we'd put things up there, and we had eggs or something, and if you ever got back in a place like this you could fry eggs. Then in the chimneys of a lot of places you'd find hams hanging up in there. And then of course a lot of people would catch chickens and kill them and cook them up. Generally when you were up on the line all you got to eat was C rations, but then when you got back for a 10-day rest you'd do most anything. Then there was one time a bunch of us guys was having fun, we'd throw these hand grenades in the creek, of course they'd go off under water and we'd get fish, clean the fish. Then we got crazy enough we was taking and unscrewing the cap and knock all the powder out, and then we'd pull the pin and toss them over to somebody. Well, they wouldn't go off. Well, I did that to one kid whose name was Bynum, I says, "Here, Quentin Bynum," well, I didn't have all the powder off so the thing exploded. It didn't have strength enough but that made us quit doing that stuff. He could have got hit in the face or something.

Then another thing, when we were back in bivouac area, they'd set up a shower out in the field, and they'd come in with a big tanker truck of water and they'd set these showers up, and then you'd go into a place and you're in the field, and you lay your other clothes there, and take a shower. And them Frenchmen would come in, especially the women, and grab your clothes and away they'd run. And then another great thing, what really got me, is maybe we'd be sitting out there and you'd dig a slit trench, and women and girls and men and everything would come up and shake your hand when you're sitting on one. You know, it's just different, comical things like that that you remember.

Like I say, I never got a, I came out of it very fortunate, and there were some good memories and that.

Aaron Elson: Ruby Goldstein talked about taking the tank and digging up potatoes. Did you ever do anything like that?

Bob Anderson: No, I know what he could do, you probably could go down a potato row like this and then pull a lever and the thing would just go like that and the potatoes would come up. See, when we went from Swindon down to Southampton there in England, this Colonel Whiteside Miller who later lost his rank, he was an oddball for being a colonel, but we'd go around corners in towns, and when you went around it you'd just tear up the curbing and everything. It cost the United States a lot of money for that run. We had to blame Miller for it. If he'd have said you have 15 hours to get down to Southampton instead of five or six hours, they wouldn't have drove and they wouldn't have been there, I think out of thirty-some tanks, I think six or seven tanks is all that made that run. The rest of them broke down. Some tore the tracks off, some did this and that. Oh, I'm telling you, that Whiteside Miller, he was something else.

Aaron Elson: Tell me about him.

Bob Anderson: Oh, I just knew him by his name. To me, he would have been a poor leader in combat. After that, then they relieved him, we got Colonel Randolph, and he was all right. And after Colonel Randolph got killed, Colonel Kedrovsky took over. I really knew Colonel Kedrovsky better than anybody, he was a really good man.

Aaron Elson: What was he like? What can you remember about him?

Bob Anderson: Well, I can't remember anything, he was just a good soldier. When he came back to the United States, he worked at Sears and Roebuck stores, and he changed his name from Colonel Kedrovsky to Kaye. He had a funny accent to his voice enough. But like I say, I really liked that man, and I've got to say that he was a good leader. And he stood behind his men. He didn't criticize some man or run him down when he did something. Well, Dixon and I were talking about, he would

30

come up and ask for advice, even enlisted men. "Now, soldier, what would we do here?" or something like that, and he'd go back and think about it. I didn't get to knowing Randolph that well.

Aaron Elson: What was the longest stretch that you ever spent inside a tank without getting out?

Bob Anderson: Oh heavens, I wouldn't have any idea.

Aaron Elson: Did you ever spend more than a day?

Bob Anderson: Oh, yes. Well, now you're saying getting out. There was times you'd get out and take a piss, something like that. But no, you'd spend a day and maybe that night sleeping on line, you'd sleep in the tank, but you're talking about getting out and walking around and that. Oh, I'd say maybe two days or three days, but still you'd get out enough. Now Hagerty, he had a lot of, I don't know what his trouble was and he'd have a lot of accidents and they'd have to bring him up clean shorts, you know, like that, whether he was too scared to get out of the tank, but he was a good man and that.

Aaron Elson: He told me a story that once you got out of the tank to take a piss, and everybody else got out, and all of a sudden shooting broke out and you had to pile back into the tank.

Bob Anderson: Yeah, shooting started, and I'd say, yeah, there'd be a lot of times when you wouldn't be done with the job, and this and that. I wonder what his favorite saying was, it was something like, "Send me up some clean underwear," or something like that. The biggest joke really with Hagerty is, he smoked, and every Lent he'd quit smoking, then after Lent he'd start smoking. And then he'd say, "God, if I could only quit that. I just wish I could quit smoking." I said, "Well, Bob, you just did for

31

six or seven weeks."

"Yeah, but that was Lent," he said. That was a big joke to me. Bob was a good man. I liked him, and like I say, I got along fine with everybody in the service and I had a good time, and still I wouldn't want to go through it again.

I had a lot more aftereffects after I got home.

Aaron Elson: Describe those.

Bob Anderson: Well, we lived a mile down the road here. I farmed for thirty years. And when I first came home, there'd be nights say that I worked in the field late, I'd be scared to go out to the barn to milk the cows because I knew there was Germans out there waiting. So I'd drive up this road right here, I knew there was a German tank, and my wife will bear that, there'd be nights I'd lay in bed and just freeze like that, she'd wake me up, and I'd be, W-w-What's the matter? "There's Germans there." I had more aftereffects, and scareder, than I did when I was over there. But I was scared, and every time after you were back on break, you'd pray that you would never have to go back up to the line. And anybody, I always said this, anybody that was in combat who wasn't scared, they're either a damn liar or they never was in combat. That's my opinion, my version of combat. If you weren't scared, you weren't in combat.

Aaron Elson: Several people have said that. Tony D'Arpino said "There's scared and there's yellow, and they're completely different."

Bob Anderson: Well, the yellowness is like I described Fowler, and Fowler admitted it, and he was a soldier because he admitted it and got out of there, because what if you'd have gone up there and you didn't have a damn round, that's what got me, if you didn't have a round of ammunition in your breech to fire, what protection did we have?

32

Aaron Elson: Did you ever see a doctor or get counseling about the aftereffects?

Bob Anderson: No. The only thing that I didn't do when I got out of the service, I think when I got home, is today I'm wearing hearing aids. If I take these off I'm stone deaf. Well, when I first got out, after a few years, I went to Iowa City, to a veterans' hospital, and they operated on my ear free of charge, but they said if I would have filled out a petition when I first got out and got my discharge, I'd have gotten free hearing aids every year. That's the only thing that I say that I did wrong. Of course, when I got back out of the service, when I landed in New York, and got back to Fort Sheridan, "How many points do you have, Soldier?" A hundred and thirty-five, I think it was, or 132. "What do you want, a discharge or a 30-day furlough?" Well, all that was on my mind was a discharge then. If I'd have taken my 30-day furlough I'd have got paid, then I'd have went back in there and stayed there ten or fifteen days more and get through that. But all I thought of was my discharge, so I got out on May 15, 1945, and I was out of the service. A lot of boys later, they took their 30-day furlough and then they came back. That was another thing that's over the river, but I could have made some money there.

A Company tanks in Bavigne, Luxembourg, during the Battle of the Bulge.

Lt. Col. Vladimir Kedrovsky

The Dillingen crossing (this sketch is of the return from Dillingen, so that the 712th Tank Battalion could go north into the Battle of the Bulge. The 90th Infantry Division burned many of the supplies it left behind so they would not fall into enemy hands.) Big Andy got his first of three Bronze Stars at Dillingen.

The Merkers salt mine, where a vast fortune in gold, currency and artworks was hidden by the Nazis. Big Andy's tank was the first to reach the mine.

The railroad tracks at Heimboldshausen, Germany, where the A Company headquarters was destroyed in an explosion.

Made in the USA
Middletown, DE
23 December 2025